Whether you are mentoring a person or a small group, Shilo Taylor has done the heavy lifting for you. Shilo's comments on her daily questions are insightful and wise. The Scripture added for each day's reading extend the content of the book for those looking to keep the discussion going. One tip: Don't skip to the core content too quickly! The small group tips in the Introduction mirror what I've taught my leaders (for decades) for small group discussions—I'd recommend turning to those over and over.

> **Sean McGever**, Young Life Area Director and
> professor of theology, Grand Canyon University

Brand New ... will refresh your heart and soul by constantly pointing you to Jesus.

> **Jarrid Wilson**, pastor and author of *Love Is Oxygen*

T0334457

BRAND NEW
MENTOR'S GUIDE

BRAND NEW MENTOR'S GUIDE

A FORTY DAY GUIDE TO LIFE IN CHRIST

SHILO TAYLOR

LEXHAM PRESS

Brand New Mentor's Guide

Copyright 2018 Shilo Taylor

Lexham Press, 1313 Commercial St., Bellingham, WA 98225
LexhamPress.com

Print ISBN 9781683591085
Digital ISBN 9781683591092

Lexham Editorial Team: Eric Bosell, Todd Hains, and Danielle Thevenaz
Cover Design: Brittany Schrock
Typesetting: ProjectLuz.com

CONTENTS

PART TWO: THE CHARACTER OF GOD

PART THREE: LIVING LIFE WITH GOD

INTRODUCTION

Whether you view yourself as a leader or not, you have the unique opportunity to walk with someone to establish a foundation of faith! You don't have to be perfect or have all the answers to be an effective leader. Your role is to continually point to Christ who is perfect and holds all the answers.

A LEADER TEACHES AND EQUIPS.

> Therefore go and make disciples of all nations, baptizing them in the name of the Father and of the Son and of the Holy Spirit, and teaching them to obey everything I have commanded you. And surely I am with you always, to the very end of the age. (Matt 28:19–20)

As you use *Brand New* as a resource to study the Bible, you will be able to facilitate discussion, add your own understanding of Scripture and experiences, and even expand on the daily readings. At the same time, remember that "I don't know, but let's find out together" is an acceptable response. Your role is to demonstrate how to ask good questions and explore the answers together. Don't be afraid to wrestle with questions and pray together as you seek answers. Your goal is to equip a new believer to study the Bible themselves and to think through what they are learning. You don't have to spoon feed them!

A LEADER DISCERNS.

> A bruised reed he will not break,
> and a smoldering wick he will not snuff out,
> till he has brought justice through to victory.
> (Matt 12:20)

This study will expose insecurities in one person, arrogance in another, and defensiveness in yet another. Through prayer and wisdom, ask what kind of disciple you have and how God would have you proceed. For example, a person dealing with shame may need you to speak indirectly with encouragement. A person who becomes defensive may need you to speak more directly and not shy away from hard questions. The Holy Spirit will give you insight as you navigate the needs of each member in the group.

A LEADER LEADS BY EXAMPLE.

> In everything set them an example by doing what is good. In your teaching show integrity, seriousness and soundness of speech that cannot be condemned, so that those who oppose you may be ashamed because they have nothing bad to say about us. (Titus 2:7–8)

We often make the mistake of thinking leading by example means we need to clean up the visible parts of our lives to look "good" to those we lead. Leading by example is much deeper than looking like you have your act together. Sharing what you have struggled with and how you have turned to Christ and his Word to transform you will speak volumes. Your own study of the Bible and your consistency in checking in and asking questions can encourage consistency in the new believer. God will use your experiences, knowledge of Scripture, and desire to seek him as you lead.

A LEADER PRAYS FOR THOSE THEY DISCIPLE.

> I thank my God every time I remember you. In all my prayers for all of you, I always pray with joy because of your partnership in the gospel from the first day until now, being confident of this, that he who began a good work in you will carry it on to completion until the day of Christ Jesus. (Phil 1:3–6)

Paul models praying over other disciples beautifully. His heart and mind were invested in other believers. He was rooting for their growth and spoke with God about them frequently. Carve out time to pray for the people you lead. Pray specifically. Ask God to reveal more of himself as they study and pray. Celebrate as God answers your prayers throughout your time together.

A LEADER TRAINS THE DISCIPLE TO DISCIPLE OTHERS.

> And the things you have heard me say in the presence
> of many witnesses entrust to reliable people who
> will also be qualified to teach others. (2 Tim 2:2)

Encourage new believers to share what God has already done in their lives. We don't have to reach a level of expertise to point to Christ! When you have completed this study of *Brand New*, ask the question, "Who can we each take through this study again?"

LEADER TIPS

As you use this daily leader guide and evaluate how to approach discussions, keep two questions in mind:

1. What is this saying?
2. How does it apply to my life?

Remember: "As iron sharpens iron, so one man sharpens another" (Prov 27:17). As a leader, God will use this study to sharpen you, too! Here are some other things to keep in mind.

Ask questions! A good leader asks questions and waits long enough for an answer to be processed and given. "How does that apply to your life now?" "What did you learn that you didn't know before?" "Why is that important?" are some starters. Avoid yes/no questions so you don't get stuck in dead-end conversations. Instead, focus on questions that start with what, how, or why.

Don't go too fast. This study provides more than just information. These are beliefs to accept and live, deep life questions to answer, and applications that aren't always easy. Give time to think and give time to see change.

Be okay with silence. In fact, expect it! It might feel like forever, but allow time for thinking, verbalizing, and courage to share. If you find yourself becoming uncomfortable or impatient, silently count to fifteen before offering another prompt.

Encourage further study. If a disciple is curious about a certain topic, feel free to explore it more before moving on to the next day of study.

Be flexible. If the first question of the day is too hard or personal to answer, start with another one and then come back to the harder question at the end.

Limit distractions. Put away phones and meet in a room that can be quiet. If you're meeting via phone, pick a time to call when distractions will be minimal.

Guide group discussion. Don't accept a wrong answer for fear of offending. If there is a wrong response, you can ask the person to state the verse or phrase that prompted their response. If a person often gives wrong answers and you need to correct it, be sure to look for opportunities to affirm them when they give a correct answer.

Be discerning. Some questions in this devotional have a right answer that can be found in Scripture. Other questions are more subjective. Ask God to give you wisdom as you help your disciple navigate their own beliefs and experiences with absolute truth.

There aren't always right answers. Use the answers in the leader guide as prompts if needed. It is not necessary to reference these answers in discussion. When the answer given is sufficient, don't try to add to it or make the disciple feel like what they said wasn't enough.

God's word is powerful. Encourage group members to highlight their Bible, take notes in the margins of their Bible, or post verses somewhere visible as a reminder.

Use your stories to encourage others to share theirs. If it is hard for a disciple to share, start sharing a little of your own experience. But do not dominate the time.

HOW TO USE *BRAND NEW*

You can lead this study many different ways, whether you are leading an individual or a small group. Here are a few ideas:

- Do each of the forty days together, consecutively. You can read it together, or you can check in daily to go over the questions in the book.
- Do the devotional for forty consecutive days, but check in weekly. Use check in time to do a day together and discuss questions throughout the week's worth of readings.
- Do one day together each week and use the devotional over forty weeks instead of forty days. Provide the

participants the additional Scripture readings listed in the leader's guide so each day can be discussed and studied more thoroughly.

"Even when I am old and gray, do not forsake me, my God, till I declare your power to the next generation, your mighty acts to all who are to come." (Ps 71:18)

LAMENTATIONS
3:22-23

Because of the Lord's great love we are not consumed, for his compassions never fail. They are new every morning; great is your faithfulness.

THE JOURNEY BEGINS

Today's focus is on a new journey of faith: looking forward to what God will do as we intentionally pursue a relationship with him. Believing in Jesus is more than a one-time decision: it is a complete life change.

READ

Answer these questions after reading John 3:16–21.

1. *What are you excited about in your journey with God?*

    Share words that describe your own feelings about your faith journey. If it is easier to think of what you are hopeful for, looking forward to, or happy about, discuss those. This is also an opportunity to discuss where your disciple is in their faith journey. Are they at a starting point? Wanting to grow in a faith they've grown up with?

2. *What scares you about your journey with God?*

   Allow the group to share their fears without providing immediate answers. Assure them that studying together can help to address many fears and unknowns. If you have a specific verse that has encouraged you, share it, but don't be nervous about letting questions sit.

3. *According to John 3:17, why did Jesus come to earth?*

   To save the world.

4. *How do Jesus' words in this passage comfort you?*

   Encourage various answers. It may be comforting that God loved the world, that we can have eternal life, that believing in Christ is enough (and my own good deeds aren't), or that Jesus is light.

FOR FURTHER STUDY

Matthew 4:18-20; Romans 8:35-39; Colossians 2:13-15.

WHAT DOES FREEDOM REALLY MEAN?

Freedom is only found in forgiveness and life in Jesus. Today we are breaking down the idea that freedom means doing what I want and not having to submit to authority. We are changing our thinking to understand that every pursuit of freedom outside of Christ results in slavery.

READ

Answer these questions after reading John 8:31–36.

1. *What are some things you have been a "slave" to?*

   You may give prompts or examples from your own life, but don't dominate the conversation. Be sure to give the disciple plenty of time to reflect and respond. Answers may vary from addictions, to feelings of worthlessness, to relationships that aren't centered on God.

2. *Describe what you think it means to be a "slave to sin" (John 8:34).*

   When we are slaves to sin, we are unable to stop sinning and have no power in ourselves to change.

3. *According to verse 32, what will the truth do?*

   The truth will set us free!

4. *How does it feel to know that you are God's child whom he has set free?*

   Ask about times of experiencing freedom in God. A possible follow-up conversation could be: If you don't feel or believe you are free yet, what is causing that block? Speak and pray the truth together using John 3:16–17 and John 8:31–36.

FOR FURTHER STUDY

Romans 6:11–18; Galatians 4:1–7, 5:1; Hebrews 2:14–15.

WHY IS THE BIBLE IMPORTANT?

The Bible is not just another book. It is the perfect, complete, alive, inspired Word of God. It is the story of the ultimate rescue: God comes down to redeem and rescue his people from sin and slavery, ending in happily ever after as we spend eternity with him. We believe that the Bible will transform our lives as the Holy Spirit speaks through it to us.

READ

Answer these questions after reading Psalm 1 and Psalm 119:105–12.

1. *What phrases does the psalmist use to describe God's word?*

   A lamp to his feet, a light to his path, and his heritage forever.

2. *In what ways do you think God's word is like a light that illuminates your path?*

   It guides, tells us how to live, gives us hope for our future, offers wisdom for today.

3. *What Bible verses or passages have you read or heard that encouraged you and brought you joy?*

   The verse you choose doesn't have to be from today's devotion. Be prepared to share a verse that sticks out in your own mind.

4. *Write down a verse that encourages you and post it where you will read it every day (nightstand, mirror, in the car, your phone lock screen).*

   Do this one with your disciple. Follow up in a couple of weeks—have they been reading it? Memorized it?

FOR FURTHER STUDY

Psalm 119:105; Isaiah 55:11; Romans 15:4; Revelation 5:9–12.

PART ONE

THE STORY OF
THE BIBLE

GOD'S CREATIVITY FROM THE BEGINNING

Today we will look at God's power, his creativity, and his perfection as he designed and spoke our world into existence. These passages in Genesis should impact our view of creation and should help us understand our value as people made in the image of God.

READ

Answer these questions after reading Genesis 1–2.

1. *What do you think it means to be created in God's image?*

   God created us to reflect him! God gave us things to care for and a mind to think with. He made us male and female. He made us for relationship.

2. *In what ways does God interact with his creation in these verses?*

   He speaks it into existence and speaks to it. He blesses it. He is generous, giving Adam and Eve food, animals, jobs, a home. He gives boundaries to Adam and Eve, telling them what they can and can't eat.

3. *What are some of the specific things that God created?*

Light, day and night, waters and land, stars and sky, vegetation, animals, humankind.

4. *What can we learn about God from observing his creation?*

We can learn many things about his character through his creation. We see he is powerful. He is above all created things, not equal to them. He is good and kind. He is creative.

FOR FURTHER STUDY

Job 12:7-10; Psalm 19:1, 96:11-12; John 1:3.

ROMANS 8:26

The Spirit himself intercedes for us through wordless groans.

OUR CHOICE

We can all identify with Adam and Eve: believing we know better than God, believing God is holding out on us, and consulting ourselves instead of God. The fall of humankind wasn't "just eating some fruit"; it was much deeper. It is important for us to see how we also struggle and sin as Adam and Eve did. We all need a Savior!

READ

Answer these questions after reading Genesis 3.

1. *Have you ever decided that you knew better than God? If so, describe the situation. What were the results?*

   Perhaps the results are visible consequences—damaged trust, broken relationships, or other issues—but also consider consequences that aren't so obvious. Did it harden your heart toward God? Did it bring guilt and shame?

2. *Why did Eve decide to eat the fruit? (See Genesis 3:6.) Do you think looks can be deceiving? Why or why not?*

Eve saw that the tree looked good and desirable for gaining wisdom. We often think looks are deceiving for other people, but believe we see clearly. We don't see that we've been deceived into believing our sin is justified or not a big deal.

3. *Who initiated the relational connection after the sin: Adam and Eve, or God? (See Genesis 3:8-9.) Why do you think that is significant?*

God initiated the relational connection. We are prone to run away from God when sin divides us from him. God approaches us and makes a way for us.

4. *How does Genesis 3:21 show God's love for us?*

He made garments of skin and clothed them. God made the first animal sacrifice to cover the naked shame of Adam and Eve. This act not only shows his tremendous love for his people even in the midst of their sin, but it also foreshadows the ceremonial sacrifices the Israelites would later adopt to cover sin and the sacrifice of Jesus to remove our sins permanently.

FOR FURTHER STUDY

Genesis 2:16-17, 3:8-11; Romans 5:12-16.

THE LIFE IS IN THE BLOOD

Sacrifice can be difficult to understand, but when we understand the principles behind sin and sacrifice, we begin to understand why Jesus' death was necessary. Leave room for questions and explore the answers together.

READ

Answer these questions after reading Leviticus 9:1–24 and Hebrews 9.

1. *What are some things you have done to try to earn God's love? Why?*

    This can connect to ways we try to earn approval from others, too. What do you try to hide from God (or what are things you won't talk about with him) to make yourself look better?

2. *How do you handle guilt and shame?*

   This can vary from hurting ourselves and wallowing in self-pity to trying harder and ignoring the guilt. It may help to ask, "What do you tell yourself when you've failed?"

3. *Why do you think God commanded the Israelites to offer animal sacrifices? (Heb 9:22-23.)*

   Without the shedding of blood, there is no forgiveness. It was the way to cover their sins.

4. *In what ways was Christ's sacrifice of himself better than the animal sacrifices?*

   It would remove sin forever, once and for all. "Christ was sacrificed once to take away the sins of many" (Heb 9:28).

FOR FURTHER STUDY

Genesis 9:4-6; Leviticus 17:10-14.

PSALM 27:1

The Lord is my light and my salvation—whom shall I fear?

THE NIGHT THE LORD PASSED OVER

The Passover ties animal sacrifice and rescue together: it foreshadows Jesus' sacrifice and ultimate rescue. We should see ourselves in the Israelites—God's people who need rescue and are ready to respond to God's rescue plan.

READ

Answer these questions after reading Exodus 12.

1. *What do God's actions in Exodus 12 tell you about his character?*

   God is powerful. God follows through with his promises. God rescues.

2. *How does this passage reveal both God's justice (v. 12) and also his mercy (v. 13)?*

   God reveals his justice by bringing judgment on all the gods of Egypt and giving consequences to the Egyptians (striking down the firstborns). God reveals his mercy by passing over all who put blood on their doorposts. The plague won't reach his people.

3. *Based on what you read in Exodus 12, why do you think John the Baptist calls Jesus "the Lamb of God" (John 1:29)?*

The lamb in Exodus was sacrificed so the firstborn would be spared and the Israelites could escape slavery. Jesus was sacrificed so all would be spared from sin and death. God's judgment passes over us when Jesus' blood has forgiven us, just like God passes over the households whose doorposts are covered with lamb's blood.

4. *What is Jesus called in 1 Corinthians 5:7? Why is that significant?*

Jesus is called the Passover lamb that has been sacrificed. Even when the Israelites are escaping Egypt, God shows he has a plan to later send his Son. We are passed over and rescued!

FOR FURTHER STUDY

Exodus 13:11–16; Romans 3:23–26.

THE LAW AND THE WILDERNESS WALK

Today's reading shows two things. First, we learn about God's law. God gives us his law because he knows what is best for our lives (he created us!). It also reveals his holiness and our inability to achieve holiness on our own. Second, we will get a glimpse into the Israelites' long journey. God uses our journeys to draw us closer to him.

READ

Answer these questions after reading Exodus 20.

1. *Why would God's presence have been frightening to the Israelites?*

    They saw thunder and lightning, heard a trumpet blast, and saw smoke. He is holy and perfect. Before him they felt the full weight of his mighty power and their sin was fully revealed. (They had also seen his power and his justice with the Egyptians.)

2. *Do you think God's presence is frightening now? Why or why not?*

This is a good time to listen. Don't worry about having the "right" answer.

3. *In what ways are the Ten Commandments good for us?*

God knows what is best for us and our lives. His commandments give us boundaries and principles for living our lives with his priorities.

4. *What do the Ten Commandments reveal to us about God's character?*

He is just. He is holy. He cares about us and our lives.

FOR FURTHER STUDY

Exodus 13:17–14:31, 15:22–27, 16, 17:1–7; Leviticus 11:44; Numbers 13–14; Matthew 22:37–40.

THE PLAN FORETOLD

Today we are learning about the prophecies of Jesus' life, death, and resurrection in Isaiah 52–53. In prophecy we see God's sovereignty even in small details. God is consistent and a keeper of promises, and his plans are set long before they play out.

READ

Answer these questions after reading Isaiah 52:13–53:12.

1. *What does it mean that all our sins were laid on Jesus? (See Isaiah 53:6.)*

   He died for all of our sins. He experienced all the consequences that we should have experienced.

2. *In what ways can you identify with the statement: "We all, like sheep, have gone astray" (Isaiah 53:6)?*

   While we can all acknowledge that "I am a sinner and I wandered away from God," this will look different for each person. Mentor, listen carefully, and discern whether you should encourage or exhort.

3. *How does this passage help you understand your sin and Jesus' sacrifice?*

   This passage is sobering and the imagery is powerful. Talk about specific verses in relation to Jesus' sacrifice.

4. *What are some of the results of Jesus' death, according to Isaiah 53:10–12?*

   He will see his offspring and prolong his days. The will of the Lord will prosper in his hand. He will see the light of life and be satisfied. He will justify many and bear their iniquities. He will divide the spoils with the strong.

FOR FURTHER STUDY

Psalm 22:16–18; Isaiah 8; Jeremiah 31; Ezekiel 36:24–30; Zechariah 12:10; Matthew 24:36–44; 1 Thessalonians 4:13–5:3; Revelation 1:7–8.

COLOSSIANS 1:17

He is before all things, and in him all things hold together.

THE PLAN UNFOLDS

This is not a story only reserved for Christmas! The birth of Jesus is God's incredible plan set in motion. It is the powerful answer to years of prophecy and faith while also being the quiet, humble beginning of Jesus living among his people.

READ

Answer these questions after reading Luke 1–2.

1. *What were the circumstances surrounding Jesus' birth? If you were God, looking for a place for your own Son to be born on earth, would you have chosen this situation? Why or why not?*

   Discuss any circumstances that stood out. As usual, God's plans were very different than anyone expected.

2. *What do you think the shepherds thought when they saw the angels? How does their response to the angel's announcement serve as an example for us?*

   They were terrified. They may have been confused or

shocked. They listened and believed the good news. They hurried to find him! Do we hurry to seek Jesus? Are we excited about what God is doing?

3. *What would you have thought about Jesus if you saw him as a baby?*

   Take a few minutes to imagine what it would be like to know you are looking at God, yet in a humble form of a baby in a manger. Remind the group how helpless babies are: "What were you able to do on your own as an infant? Is it hard for you to imagine God as an infant? Why or why not?"

4. *What did you learn in these verses about God's plan?*

   Relate this back to God's plan in our own lives. Is it hard to trust God's plan when we don't know how it will play out? How does knowing God's plan in sending Jesus impact your view of God's plan for your life, personally?

FOR FURTHER STUDY

Matthew 1; John 1:1–18; 2 Corinthians 3:18.

REPENT, FOR THE KINGDOM OF HEAVEN HAS COME NEAR

"Or do you show contempt for the riches of his kindness, forbearance and patience, not realizing that God's kindness is intended to lead you to repentance?" (Rom 2:4). God has been kind, leading us to realize our sinfulness and need for him. Today is a personal focus, looking at our own need for repentance.

READ

Answer these questions after reading 2 Corinthians 7:2–16.

1. *How would you define repentance?*

   "Godly sorrow brings repentance that leads to salvation and leaves no regret, but worldly sorrow brings death" (2 Cor 7:10). Repentance is turning away from our sin and turning toward Jesus' forgiveness.

2. *What do you need to repent of? In what areas do you need God's strength to help you change?*

After everyone has an opportunity to share, pause to pray specifically for these areas that were identified. Don't make light or move quickly through this question, but do affirm and encourage that God's forgiveness is complete.

3. *Have you ever experienced "godly sorrow" over a sin? If so, describe the situation.*

   Worldly sorrow can lead to feeling guilt, shame, and beating ourselves up. Godly sorrow is conviction from the Holy Spirit to turn away from our sin and toward Jesus. Godly sorrow has hope and trust that God can transform us. Mentors, be patient, as it may be difficult to identify and work through repentance. Listen carefully to discern if any of the members in your group is struggling with worldly sorrow or godly sorrow.

4. *According to 2 Corinthians 7:10, what is the result of repentance?*

   Repentance doesn't leave us in sorrow; it leads us to salvation. We may still have to face the consequences of our sin, but we have a Savior who will walk with us no matter what happens.

FOR FURTHER STUDY

Ezekiel 18:30-32; Matthew 3:1-12; Mark 1:1-8; Luke 15:7.

JESUS IS ONE PERSON, FULLY GOD AND FULLY HUMAN

Before reading Hebrews 4–5 today, explain that the high priest was the priest responsible for making sacrifices and interceding on behalf of the people. Jesus is our sacrifice and intercedes before the Father on our behalf. He is our high priest, and he is fully God.

READ

Answer these questions after reading Hebrews 4:14–5:10.

1. *In what ways is Jesus able to empathize with us?*

   He has been tempted in every way (Heb 4:15).

2. *Why can we approach the throne of grace more confidently when we know that Jesus can empathize with us?*

   He understands and has mercy for us, but he also is perfect. We can trust his judgment and promises.

3. *How should it affect your daily frustrations and joys to*
    know that Jesus experienced everything you are facing—
    sin, doubt, fear, joy?

    Being understood and known is important to us as
    people. Emphasize Jesus' empathy toward us.

4. *What do you learn about Jesus' prayer life in Hebrews 5:7?*

    He values prayer and modeled obedience. Even he
    poured out his heart to the Father.

FOR FURTHER STUDY

Luke 3:22; 2 Corinthians 5:21; Colossians 2:8-10; 1 Peter 1:18-19.

PSALM 51:10

Create in me a pure heart, O God, and renew a steadfast spirit within me.

JESUS' MINISTRY ON EARTH

Today's study provides an overview of the struggle, perfection, and sacrifice of Jesus' life. We can identify with Jesus' life but also recognize that unlike us, he lived God's will perfectly.

READ

Answer these questions after reading Matthew 4:1–11; Mark 2:1–12; Mark 7; Mark 8.

1. *How does it help you to know Jesus was tempted too?*

   He understands our struggles with temptation. He models how to fight temptation.

2. *How does Jesus use Scripture? In what ways could you apply that practice in your own life?*

   He uses Scripture to fight temptation. He knows it well enough to identify when Satan is twisting it. He uses it to show how he will fulfill Scripture and to proclaim truth to the religious people.

3. *Why do you think the powerful political and religious leaders felt threatened by Jesus?*

   He spoke with authority and called their legalism into question. He spoke as God but they didn't believe he was God.

4. *Over what and whom does Jesus have power?*

   Everything and everyone! He has power over Satan. He has power to forgive sins and to heal.

FOR FURTHER STUDY

Four gospels are devoted to the life of Jesus but only one day in *Brand New*. If you can spend more time reading about Jesus' life on earth, here are a few places to start:

- Jesus' baptism (Matt 3:13–17).
- Satan took advantage of this high point to tempt Jesus (Matt 4:1–11).
- Jesus returned from the wilderness, preaching the kingdom of God, casting out demons, and performing miracles (Luke 4:16–44).
- Jesus chose disciples, sending them out to proclaim the kingdom and perform miracles (Luke 6:12–16; 9:1–6).

- God's blessing, the law, prayer, judgment, and truth (Matt 5–7).
- Jesus commanded demons to flee (Mark 5:1–20), wind and weather to be calm (Luke 8:22–25), the blind to see (Mark 10:46–51), the deaf and mute to hear and to speak (Mark 7:31–37), and the dead to rise (John 11:38–44).
- His message and might made the powerful uncomfortable and suspicious of him (John 11:45–57).
- He revealed the hypocrisy of the religious elite (Mark 12:38–44).
- He drove out merchants and moneychangers (Luke 19:45–47).
- He warned his followers that he would die, but that they should not fear; he would rise from the dead (Mark 8:31; 9:30–31; 10:32–34).
- He declares his essential identity as "the way" (John 14:6).
- He offers to bear our burdens and provide rest to all (Matt 11:28).

JESUS' DEATH ON THE CROSS

It's a somber day. Jesus' sacrifice came at a cost. Today we look at the betrayal, the false accusations, the chaos, the humiliation, the excruciating physical pain, and the miraculous events within it. God's hand was at work even when it all appeared to be falling apart. This is true of our lives, too— God is at work, even when nothing seems to be going right.

READ

Answer these questions after reading Matthew 26–27.

1. *Why do you think Peter struggled to accept God's plan?*

   It wasn't what Peter pictured. Review Matthew 26:33–35 and 51 to get an idea of what Peter may have expected. Peter was thinking about himself and his own resolve, not God's bigger plan.

2. *According to Matthew 26:56, how did Jesus' disciples respond to his arrest?*

They deserted him and fled.

3. *What impacted you most today as you read about Jesus' crucifixion in Matthew 27?*

Be patient. Encourage the group to share specific verses that stood out or an overall theme.

4. *What convinced the guards that Jesus was the Son of God in Matthew 27:54?*

The curtain was torn in two from top to bottom, the earth shook, rocks split, tombs broke open, people were raised to life.

FOR FURTHER STUDY

Matthew 16:21–22; 17:22–23; 20:17–19; 20:20–28; Hebrews 2:14–15; 1 Peter 2:21–25.

JESUS' RESURRECTION

Hooray! We've reached the resurrection! Today is a day of celebration. Jesus' resurrection should impact our daily life. It should change our perspective and influence the choices we make. It is the hope we have for the future.

READ

Answer these questions after reading John 20.

1. *According to John 20:19-20, how did the disciples feel before they saw the resurrected Jesus? How did they feel after they saw Jesus?*

   Before they saw the resurrected Jesus, they were fearful and hiding (see also Luke 24:19-23). After they saw the resurrected Jesus, they were overjoyed (see also Luke 24:30-32).

2. *How do Jesus' words in John 20:29 encourage you?*

   There is no right answer. Encourage personal accounts.

3. *Why is Jesus' resurrection important? What did Jesus accomplish by rising from the dead?*

It means he was the perfect sacrifice and defeated death itself. He fulfilled prophecy.

4. *If you believe Jesus died and rose again, how should that impact your life? How should it impact your decisions and actions?*

It should change everything! We have freedom instead of guilt and shame. We have a relationship with God himself. We have hope for true life.

FOR FURTHER STUDY

John 3:16–17; 1 Corinthians 15:54–55; Colossians 2:13–15.

REVELATION 21:4-5

"He will wipe every tear from their eyes. There will be no more death or mourning or crying or pain, for the old order of things has passed away." He who was seated on the throne said, "I am making everything new!"

JESUS' ASCENSION

Jesus' ascension is important to us as believers. It was the end and fulfillment of his earthly work. He was alive and he left the earth alive! He then returned to heavenly glory, and yet he continues to minister to his church through the Holy Spirit. He also promises to prepare a place for us with him in heaven.

READ

Answer these questions after reading Luke 24:44–53.

1. *Have you ever been confused by a passage of Scripture that you couldn't understand? If so, how do Jesus' words in Luke 24:45 encourage you?*

   Remember to listen carefully and direct accordingly. God can help us understand and apply the Bible. We can ask him to direct and help us.

2. *According to Jesus, what do the Scriptures say about the Messiah?*

   Luke 24:46–47 tells us that Jesus had fulfilled Old Testament prophecies about the Messiah and explains that the good news of his resurrection and forgiveness would spread throughout the world.

3. *What was Jesus doing when he ascended into heaven?*

   He was blessing his disciples.

4. *How did the disciples respond when they watched Jesus be taken up into heaven?*

   Luke 24:52–53 says that they worshiped him and then returned to Jerusalem and continued to worship God at the temple.

FOR FURTHER STUDY

Daniel 7:18; Luke 24:46–47; Acts 1:1–10; Ephesians 1:18–21.

PENTECOST AND LIVING IN THE IN-BETWEEN

We live in the in-between of Jesus' death and resurrection (knowing we are secure in our salvation) and his second coming (when all will be made right and we can live eternally with him). In the in-between God has given us purpose, his promises, and his Spirit to equip us.

READ

Answer these questions after reading Acts 2.

1. *How did the disciples respond to being called drunkards, liars, and crazy people?*

   They pointed back to Jesus. They (mostly Peter) explained that the Holy Spirit was fulfilling prophecy from the book of Joel. He then gave the gospel message to the people.

2. *How do you tend to respond to people who don't agree with you?*

   You may give some direction for this: Do we defend? Do we avoid? Do we make it all about us or them? You can also discuss how Peter keeps the message of Jesus central to all he does. What things are central to our lives? What do we point to when we have conflict with others?

3. *What are some of the things that the early church did? (See Acts 2:42–47.)*

   They devoted themselves to the apostles' teaching and to the breaking of bread and prayer; they fellowshipped and ate together with glad and sincere hearts. They sold their property and possessions to give to anyone who had need. They met together in the temple courts every day. They praised God. They saw many people come to trust Jesus.

4. *According to Acts 2:47, how did God respond to the early church's faithful obedience?*

   He added to their number daily those who were being saved.

FOR FURTHER STUDY

The Holy Spirit established the church through the ministry and miracles of the disciples, which paralleled the ministry and miracles of Jesus. Read Acts 1 and Romans 8, and review the following:

- "God's love has been poured out into our hearts through the Holy Spirit, who has been given to us" (Rom 5:5).
- Christians preached the gospel in power, adding thousands to the church's number (for example, Acts 2:22–41).
- They healed the sick (Acts 5:12–16) and made cripples walk (Acts 3:1–10).
- They cast out demons (Acts 16:16–18).
- They brought the dead to life (Acts 9:36–42).
- They also suffered persecution, even to the point of death (Acts 7:54–8:1; 12:1–2) and division (Acts 15).
- The Holy Spirit comes in power in baptism and the preaching of the word (Acts 2:1–4; 8:14–17; 10:44–48).

JESUS IS COMING BACK

We can trust God's promise that he is coming back. We have so much to look forward to! Today, focus on how this impacts our lives right now. How do we live differently when we know the outcome is Jesus' return and he will make things right again?

READ

Answer these questions after reading Matthew 24.

1. *Why is it important to know the Bible and God's promises? (See Matthew 24:3–13.)*

   We need to know God's word and promises so that we aren't deceived by false prophecy or led astray worrying about world events. We need to be prepared for the trials that will come but also hold onto the hope of Jesus' promised return.

2. *Why shouldn't you be afraid of things to come? (See Matthew 24:35.)*

Heaven and earth will pass away, but God's word will not. His promises will truly come to pass.

3. *Based on Matthew 24:36, how should you respond when you hear about someone who has predicted a specific date for the end of the world?*

Know that "about that day or hour no one knows, not even the angels in heaven, nor the Son, but only the Father."

4. *How seriously do you take the job Jesus has given you to "keep watch" (Matthew 24:42)?*

Discuss what "keep watch" means to us today. Examples include reading the Bible, studying God's promises, praying about his will as his return grows closer, sharing the gospel with others, and not holding too tightly to this world but expecting Jesus to return and make all things right. In what ways does reading Matthew 24 encourage you to "keep watch"?

FOR FURTHER STUDY

Philippians 1:27; Colossians 3:3–4; 2 Peter 3; 1 John 2:17.

EXODUS 19:4

You yourselves have seen what I did to Egypt, and how I carried you on eagles' wings and brought you to myself.

HEAVEN

Our hopes, expectations, and dreams are simply not big enough to describe heaven. It will surpass any fantasy we can conjure up. Today's reading should excite you and cause you to dream bigger about how God will fulfill every need, desire, and purpose in us when we move to heaven. We will also try to clear up some misconceptions about heaven.

READ

Answer these questions after reading Revelation 21–22.

1. *What images and ideas do you think about when you picture heaven?*

   Talk about different movies, music, or Sunday School lessons that have shaped your views of heaven.

2. *How has your idea of heaven changed after reading today's Bible verses?*

   Focus on specific verses that have caused a shift in thinking.

3. *What are some of the things that will not be in heaven? (See Revelation 21:4.)*

Death, mourning, crying, and pain.

4. *What excites you about heaven?*

Think about questions you'd like answered and people you hope to see. Are you excited about what you'll see or what you'll experience? Imagine a life without sadness and anxiety. Dream big!

FOR FURTHER STUDY

Revelation 15; Isaiah 25:8–12; John 14:2–4; Revelation 7:13–17.

PART TWO

THE CHARACTER OF GOD

GOD IS A MYSTERY

Many concepts in our faith are difficult to understand. While we want to continue growing, learning, and grasping God's truth, we also want to accept the fact that we will never know it all. God is deeper than we can grasp. May this be a comfort and not a discouragement to us.

READ

Answer these questions after reading Romans 11:33–36.

1. *What did you learn about about God's wisdom?*

   It is deep, unsearchable. No one can know God's mind fully.

2. *Why do you think that no matter how much we learn about God, there is always more of God for us to know?*

   He is infinite. Our minds are finite. He is bigger in every way than we can fathom.

3. *How are you encouraged to know your relationship with God will continue to grow?*

Remind the group that we will never have everything all figured out. There will always be new things to discover. It may help them to hear that you are still growing in your own relationship with God.

4. *What new things have you learned about God in the last couple of weeks?*

If this is hard to come up with on the spot, take time to let the participants look through their answers and notes of the last few weeks. It is valuable to regularly revisit the things God is teaching us and share them with one another. It helps them stick.

FOR FURTHER STUDY

Job 11:7-9; Psalm 131, 147:5; Isaiah 40:28; Colossians 1:25-27.

GOD IS A TRINITY

The Trinity is a difficult concept for our limited minds. Christians use many analogies to try to make it easier to understand (such as the three parts of an egg making up a whole, the three sides of a triangle making up the whole). Unfortunately, each analogy falls short and can add more confusion, so we will stick to what Scripture says about the Trinity. We must also accept that we won't fully understand the Trinity mystery on this side of heaven.

READ

Answer these questions after reading Matthew 3:13–17 and Psalm 131.

1. *How can we observe all three Persons of the Trinity in Matthew 3:16–17?*

   Jesus was in the water being baptized. The Spirit came down like a dove on him. The Father's voice was heard from heaven.

2. *How is the psalmist able to find peace even though he doesn't understand everything?*

He doesn't let himself get overwhelmed but understands his knowledge is limited. He hopes in God even when he doesn't understand. A baby can be comforted and feel safe even if she doesn't understand. She trusts those who love her and care for her needs.

3. *What are some of the distinctions between God the Father, God the Son, and God the Holy Spirit?*

The Bible holds three truths together:

- There is only one true God (Isa 40:3).
- The Father, the Son, and the Spirit are each that God (John 6:27; Heb 1:1–3, 8; Acts 28:25–28).
- The Father, the Son, and the Spirit aren't each other (John 16:7–16; 2 Cor 13:14).

Only the Father has a Son and a Spirit. Only the Son has a body. Only the Spirit is sent to be the presence of God with us, dwelling in us (John 16:7–15).

4. *How do we see the unity of God the Father and God the Son and God the Holy Spirit?*

Use the same approach used in question 3 about how we think and speak of God. Together the Father, Son, and Spirit do all things: create (Gen 1:1–3; Col 1:15–17), save (John 16–17; 1 Pet 1:2), and make holy (John 17:16–21; 1 Thess 5:23).

FOR FURTHER STUDY

Matthew 1:23, 28:19–20; John 10:30, 14:8–9; 1 Corinthians 8:6; 2 Corinthians 1:21–22; Ephesians 4:4–6; 1 Peter 1:1–2.

MATTHEW 12:20

A bruised reed he will not break, and a smoldering wick he will not snuff out.

GOD IS THE ONLY GOD

Our world may want to believe there are many gods we can worship, but Scripture affirms God is the only God and he is the only one worthy of our worship. What does that look like in our lives?

READ

Answer these questions after reading Isaiah 44:6–8 and 45:5–7.

1. *What do you think it means that God is the first and the last? (See Isaiah 44:6.)*

    God exists outside of time—he created it! He encompasses its beginning and end. He was there before time existed and he will exist forever. He's the only one that is past, present, and future.

2. *What things—relationships, objects, goals—have you put in a place ahead of God?*

Point out that idols aren't only statues to worship. Idol worship can take many forms in our lives. It may be easy to understand that God is the only God to worship. It may be harder to identify the things we put in his place.

3. *How does God answer the question, "Is there any God besides me?" (See Isaiah 44:8.)*

"No, there is no other Rock; I know not one."

4. *According to Isaiah 45:7, what are some of the things God is in control of in this life?*

God is in control of light, darkness, prosperity, and disaster.

FOR FURTHER STUDY

Deuteronomy 6:4–5; Isaiah 42:8; Zechariah 14:9; 1 Timothy 2:5–6; Revelation 1:8.

GOD IS EVERYWHERE AND GOD KNOWS EVERYTHING

God knowing everything and being everywhere might bring comfort ("I'm so glad to be known and that there are no surprises to God") or fear ("I can't escape him! I don't want him to know everything about me"). Today may bring mixed emotions. If your disciple fears God's presence and all-knowing nature, it may be a good opportunity to revisit God's forgiveness and his desire to walk with us in every area of our lives.

READ

Answer these questions after reading Romans 8:26–39.

1. *What verse from today meant the most to you? Why?*

   This is a great opportunity to remind the group to highlight verses that stood out to them, or to post them somewhere for a daily, visible reminder. Ask them how they can remember it best.

2. *Have you ever tried to escape God? If so, what happened?*

If it is hard for a participant to talk about this, share a little of your own experience. Please remember to model answering this question, and don't monopolize the discussion.

3. *How does knowing that God sees all and knows all affect your relationship with him?*

Be sensitive. This question might bring shame and fear to those who feel a need to hide from God. You may need to remind them of other aspects of God's character: he is not surprised by anything, his love is unconditional, he is willing to forgive, and so forth.

4. *Is there a situation in your life that is frustrating or disappointing to you? If so, how does the truth of Romans 8:28 affect your perspective of that situation?*

Spend some time praying about this situation.

FOR FURTHER STUDY

Psalm 69:5, 139:7–12; Proverbs 15:3; Romans 11:33–34; 1 Corinthians 2:9–11.

GOD IS LOVE THAT WON'T FADE

There aren't many things we can depend on to remain unchanged regardless of circumstance, emotion, and time. Today's discussion about love should focus us on our identity as God's beloved and on the way his love moves us to love others in the same unconditional way.

READ

Answer these questions after reading 1 John 4:7–21.

1. *What did you learn in this passage about God's love for you?*

   You can also compare the love celebrated in 1 John to the "love" we see in our world today, which is often based on impulse and assumes that the purpose of relationships is to fulfill ourselves.

2. *In what ways do you tend to respond to God's love?*

We can be accepting and appreciative of love but sometimes we have a hard time accepting what we haven't "earned." Do we accept and love God back or do we respond with unbelief, hesitancy, or even defensiveness?

You may extend this question to discuss people in our lives who have shown us God's love. How was this love displayed? What was our response to the person demonstrating unconditional love to us?

3. *How does God's love impact your life?*

Make this as practical as you can. Love impacts our feelings and beliefs, but it should also be evident in our actions. How will God's love impact what you do in the next seven days?

4. *Why must Christians love each other? (See 1 Corinthians 13.)*

Love is how others know what God is like. God loved us first and calls us to extend the same love to each other. Without love, we are like a clanging cymbal—a lot of noise but nothing worth listening to.

FOR FURTHER STUDY

Psalm 86:15, 136:26; Ephesians 2:4–5; 1 Peter 5:7.

PSALM 139:12

*Even the darkness will not be dark
to you; the night will shine like the
day, for darkness is as light to you.*

GOD IS PERFECT AND UNCHANGING

Psalm 18:30 reminds us that "As for God, his way is perfect: the Lord's word is flawless; he shields all who take refuge in him," and Hebrews 13:8 explains that "God is perfect and the same yesterday, today and forever." Knowing this should influence how we see our current circumstances. Learning about God's character should deepen our trust in him.

READ

Answer these questions after reading Psalm 18.

1. *What did you learn in this psalm about God's reliability?*

   Psalm 18 is full of rescue! God answers when his people call to him. Contrasting God's reliability with human reliability will be helpful.

2. *When have you trusted God to be perfect and unchanging?*

   Psalm 18 is full of hope in God's perfect faithfulness. If a group member shares that he or she hasn't trusted

God in this way yet, ask how such trust might change his or her perspective on current circumstances.

3. *Why do you think this psalm compares God to a rock?*

He is immovable, unchanging, solid.

4. *How does the psalmist respond to God's perfect, unchanging character?*

He loves God. He calls out to him for help. He keeps God's laws. He trusts God. He has courage to do battle. He praises him. Encourage reflection on God's character.

FOR FURTHER STUDY

Deuteronomy 32:4; 2 Samuel 22:31; Psalm 19:7–11, 92:15, 102:27; Hebrews 13:8.

GOD IS A REFUGE

Our safe place, our refuge, is not found in things or people. Our refuge is found in God. You've already read about how trustworthy and unchanging God is. These characteristics of God cause us to trust him with our circumstances. We get to apply our growing trust today!

READ

Answer these questions after reading Psalm 46.

1. *What do you need strength to face today?*

   Be patient and remind the group that no challenge is too insignificant. There may be huge obstacles or some seemingly small aspect of their day. Do not minimize anything they are facing.

2. *What fears or struggles do you need to trust God to be your refuge for?*

   This is an opportunity to talk with the disciple about any obstacles that are preventing them from trusting God as their refuge. Speak and pray God's word over any fears or wrong beliefs that are preventing them from trusting him.

3. *How does knowing that God is your strength affect your view of difficult situations? (See Psalm 46:2–3.)*

   Note that in Psalm 46, God doesn't promise to stop difficult situations from happening in this life. He demonstrates that he is present and working within them.

4. *In what areas of your life do you need to "Be still, and know that [he is] God" (Psalm 46:10)?*

   Challenge your group to implement this today! Encourage each of them to take time to be still and know that he is God.

FOR FURTHER STUDY

Deuteronomy 33:27; Psalm 91:2; Proverbs 14:26; Isaiah 25:4.

GOD IS THE ULTIMATE WARRIOR

God has unmatched strength, victory, and power. Not only will he reign for eternity, but we are also invited to take part in the battle and the victory. We don't get to stay neutral, so use today's study to become battle ready.

READ

Answer these questions after reading Ephesians 6:10–20.

1. *Compare and contrast spiritual armor with military armor.*

    Instead of our own strength, we depend on God's strength in prayer, through his word, and by his Holy Spirit. Instead of literal breastplates, shields, helmets, and weapons, we rely on righteousness, the gospel of peace, faith, salvation, the Holy Spirit, and the Word of God.

2. *How should you prepare for spiritual battles in your life?*

We prepare for spiritual battle through prayer, reading the Bible, and spending time with other believers who support us.

3. *Who is the enemy that you are fighting in these spiritual battles? (Ephesians 6:12.)*

The rulers, authorities, powers of the world, and spiritual forces of evil—that is, sin, the world, the devil, and his minions.

4. *What changes do you need to make in your life in order to "be alert and always keep on praying for the Lord's people" (Ephesians 6:28)?*

Be as specific as possible. What changes can be implemented today?

FOR FURTHER STUDY

2 Corinthians 10:3–5; 1 Thessalonians 5:6–8; Hebrews 4:12–13.

LUKE 1:38

"I am the Lord's servant. ... May your word to me be fulfilled."

GOD IS FORGIVENESS

God's forgiving character allows us to repent and have restored relationship with him. For example, David had to face the consequences of his sin, but he was able to endure those consequences with God. His restored relationship with God gave him hope every step of the way.

READ

Answer these questions after reading Psalm 51.

1. *How did David respond when God exposed his sin? (See also 2 Samuel 12:13.)*

   He confessed, "I have sinned against the Lord."

2. *How do you tend to respond when God exposes your sin?*

   Mentor, be aware that there are four broad responses to sin: we deny it, we excuse it, we fear it, and we confess it. Sometimes we go through all four responses! You will need to respond to each response differently. For example, someone who denies or excuses their sin needs more frank confrontation, while someone who feels deep guilt over their sin needs to be directed to the consolation of God's promises of forgiveness. If a group member can identify which response they are prone to, discuss and pray about this together.

3. *Even though David's sin affected several people, who does he say he sinned against in Psalm 51:4? Why is that significant?*

    He says he sinned against the Lord. David recognized that first of all, breaking God's commands was rebellion against God.

4. *If the Lord is revealing sin in your life today, use David's model of repentance: acknowledge God's just and forgiving character and your sin, ask for forgiveness, ask God to change you, and thank him.*

    We may think hurting a person should be resolved between us and that person, but it also needs to be resolved between us and God. Reconciling with God should be our starting point.

FOR FURTHER STUDY

2 Samuel 11–12; Acts 3:19–20.

GOD IS PERSONAL

The God of all creation—the God who has a plan for all people, the God who promises true life—also cares deeply, intricately, and personally for each one of us. He is not detached or uninvolved. We are his creation and his children, and we should see ourselves as such.

READ

Answer these questions after reading Psalm 139.

1. *How does Psalm 139 change the way you see yourself?*

   You may want to write down the specific verses that are changing your perspective. As we study God's word, we have the opportunity to replace wrong beliefs about our identity with a better understanding of how God made and sees us.

2. *What are some unique things about you?*

   This is a celebration of how God created us in his image! If your disciple is having a hard time sharing unique aspects about themselves, point out things you see in him or her that reflect God's character and are unique and wonderful.

3. *According to Psalm 139:1–5, how well does God know you? How does that reality make you feel?*

God knows us better than anyone else. He knows our words even before we speak them.

4. *How does it impact your view of your perceived flaws to know that you are "fearfully and wonderfully made" (Psalm 139:14)?*

Encourage anyone who is critical of themselves. Remind them that God is delighted with the unique way he created them. Gently urge them to bring their insecurities and feelings of inadequacy straight to the one who made them!

FOR FURTHER STUDY

Ephesians 2:10; Deuteronomy 31:6.

PART THREE

LIVING LIFE
WITH GOD

CHURCH—A BUILDING CAN'T CONTAIN IT

Views of what church should be and what our role should be in it can vary greatly. Today we read about God's intention for his church: to bring others to salvation, to build each other up, and to wait together for his second coming. Church is not an optional part of our Christian lives—it is God's good plan for us.

READ

Answer these questions after reading Acts 2:37–47.

1. *What comes to mind when you think of a "church"?*

   This can be a combination of positive and negative connotations and memories. Listen and consider how you can respond with empathy and also with the truth that the church is God's plan for us.

2. *What did you learn about God's plan for the church in Acts 2?*

His plan is to use the church to spread the gospel and bring other people to repentance and into relationship with him. His plan is also to show his love through the church.

3. *Why is it important for you to be part of a local church?*

Here are some examples of answers: It is important to have accountability, to have other believers challenge and support us, to show God's love to others, to meet practical needs and have our needs met, or to be a part of what God is doing on earth. These are just a few reasons—keep listing your own!

4. *If you are part of a local church, in what ways is your church similar to the church in Acts 2? How is it different?*

This is not a time to be critical, but a time to step back to see what God intended for the church. How can we contribute in a way that reflects God's purpose for the church?

FOR FURTHER STUDY

Romans 12:3–8; 1 Corinthians 12; Ephesians 4.

MALACHI 4:2

The sun of righteousness will
rise with healing in its rays.

BAPTISM—IT'S NOT JUST WATER

If baptism is a new concept, do not pressure ("You need to be baptized!") but encourage ("Let's talk and pray about this together"). If you sense reluctance, use wisdom, prayer, and patience. It may be worth revisiting at the end of the study. Today, focus on why God introduced baptism and what it means.

READ

Answer these questions after reading Matthew 3 and Colossians 2:9–3:17.

1. *What new thing did you learn about baptism?*

   This may raise new questions. Answer anyone's questions about baptism and encourage them to discuss baptism with their pastor.

2. *What is baptism a picture of? (See Colossians 2:12.)*

Just as Jesus died and was buried, in baptism, I die to my old life. Just as Jesus was raised from the dead, he raises me into a new life with him.

3. *Have you been baptized? If so, describe that experience.*

If your disciple has not been baptized, use this time to describe your own experience.

4. *If you have committed your life to Jesus but you haven't been baptized, talk to your pastor or small group leader about it.*

This is something you can do together! Go with your disciple to discuss baptism if they need some support or encouragement.

FOR FURTHER STUDY

Acts 16:31–33, 22:16; Romans 6:8–11; 1 Peter 3:21.

COMMUNION—IT'S NOT A SNACK

If possible, partake in Communion soon after completing this day's study. Communion should be taken on a regular basis as remembrance, as celebration, as spiritual nourishment, and as opportunity for self-examination.

READ

Answer these questions after reading Matthew 26:26–30.

1. *What did you learn about Communion today?*

   You can focus on this question if more needs to be answered, or move on if the information isn't new.

2. *Why do you think Communion is important?*

   Jesus commanded us to remember his life, his ministry, and his sacrifice. Jesus says in John 6:54–56, "Whoever eats my flesh and drinks my blood has eternal life, and I will raise them up at the last day. For my flesh is real food and my blood is real drink. Whoever eats my flesh and drinks my blood remains in me, and I in them."

3. *In what ways is Communion similar to the Passover meal?*

Review Exodus 12 (Day 7) if needed. When Jesus ate the Passover meal with his disciples (Matt 26), he connected that meal to his own ministry and sacrifice. First, he blessed the meal, then he took bread and said: "Take and eat; this is my body" (Matt 26:26). Then he took the cup and said: "Drink from it, all of you. This is my blood of the covenant, which is poured out for many for the forgiveness of sins" (Matt 26:27–28). Just as the Passover lamb was slain and its blood placed on the doorposts as the mark of the Israelites' salvation, so too was Jesus slain and his blood shed on the cross for our salvation.

4. *Why do you think it is important for us to examine ourselves before we take Communion?*

In 1 Corinthians 11:26–29 Paul says, "For whenever you eat this bread and drink this cup, you proclaim the Lord's death until he comes. So then, whoever eats the bread or drinks the cup of the Lord in an unworthy manner will be guilty of sinning against the body and blood of the Lord." Everyone ought to examine themselves before they eat of the bread and drink from the cup. For those who eat and drink without discerning the body of Christ eat and drink judgment on themselves. In this meal Jesus nourishes us and heals us. You may also ask, "What nourishment do you need? How do you need to be healed?"

FOR FURTHER STUDY

John 6:32–59; 1 Corinthians 11:23–32.

WORSHIP—MORE THAN SINGING

We often reduce worship to a time of singing in church, yet it is so much more than that! The core of worship is to declare who God is. May you experience freedom and creativity as you explore various ways to worship and celebrate God.

READ

Answer these questions after reading Psalm 84.

1. *In what ways does your life show you worship God?*

    The opposite could also be asked: what things in your life *prevent* worship of God? Be patient and encouraging with self-examination. This may be a time to confess and ask God to refocus us if our lives aren't reflecting worship of God.

2. *What do you think of when you hear the word "worship"?*

Today is an opportunity to broaden our idea of worship. Encourage the disciple to think about using their own gifts, passions, and personality to worship God.

3. *Have you ever had a strong desire to praise and worship God? (See Psalm 84:1–2.) If so, describe that experience.*

Share your own experience. What has prompted you to praise and worship God? You can point out how David expressed his desire to worship in the Psalms.

4. *Ask God how he wants you to worship him today.*

Reminder: worship is not about us. Time with God can be spent in many ways, but worship is specifically adoring, revering, and praising God for who he is and what he has done.

FOR FURTHER STUDY

1 Chronicles 16:23–36; John 4:21–24; Acts 2:42–47; Romans 12:1–2; Revelation 4:8–11.

ROMANS 8:39

[Nothing] will be able to separate us from the love of God that is in Christ Jesus our Lord.

PRAYER—TALKING WITH GOD

The Bible frequently speaks about prayer. Our focus today is to grow in our own prayer life. Look at how David poured everything out to the Lord instead of becoming overwhelmed by his circumstance. His honesty and focus on God resulted in a deep, conversational prayer life.

READ

Answer these questions after reading Psalm 31.

1. *What words or phrases stood out to you as you read David pouring out his concerns to God?*

   Together, highlight or underline a favorite phrase in your Bibles.

2. *What phrases does David use to acknowledge who God is?*

   He calls God his rock, refuge, and strong fortress.

3. *When David called to God for help (Psalm 31:22), how did God respond?*

   He heard David's cry for mercy. Note: This may raise questions about when God doesn't seem to respond to prayer. Don't be afraid of hard questions like this. Even if God doesn't seem to answer prayers the way we hope, he answers prayer by drawing us into a deeper relationship with him and shaping us into people after his heart.

4. *Today find a prayer spot—a quiet place, free of distraction, where you can focus on God as you pray.*

FOR FURTHER STUDY

1 Kings 8:27–30; 1 Chronicles 16:11; Ephesians 6:18; James 5:13–16; 1 John 5:14–15.

GIVING—WHAT WE DO WITH WHAT WE HAVE

We give to the Lord because everything comes from him. We acknowledge that we are dependent and thankful for his provision and gifts. We don't give out of guilt, expectation of getting more in return, or obligation. Let's focus on how we offer all areas of our life up to God for his use, not just our money.

READ

Answer these questions after reading Mark 12:38–44.

1. *Why did Jesus warn against the teachers of the law?*

   They show off, acting pompous and prestigious as if they're holy because they give. They make a show of wealth and pious-sounding prayers while taking advantage of the poor.

2. *How much did the widow give to God?*

   She gave two small copper coins, worth only a few pennies.

3. *Why was the widow's gift considered more than all the others? (See Mark 12:43-44.)*

   Everyone else gave out of their wealth. It was no sacrifice. But the widow gave everything she had. She made a true sacrifice.

4. *What are some specific ways that you can dedicate your time, talents, and possessions to the Lord? Commit now to what you will give him.*

   You can discuss time, talents, and possessions, or choose one to focus on. When you commit to something, make sure it is tangible and clear. Decide now if this is something you want to revisit after a certain amount of time.

FOR FURTHER STUDY

Psalm 37:21; Proverbs 11:25, 18:16; Matthew 6:1-4; 2 Corinthians 9:6-13.

SERVICE—BEING ABOUT MORE THAN YOURSELF

In Matthew 5 we are called the light of the world. When our light shines before others, they may see our good deeds and glorify God. We have the privilege of showing others who God is in the way we serve and treat them.

READ

Answer these questions after reading John 13:1-17.

1. *When have other people gone out of their way to serve you? Describe the circumstances.*

   You can extend this to ask, "How did being served make you feel?" Sometimes being served is a relief and blessing, and sometimes we have a hard time receiving the blessing.

2. *Why do you think Jesus says, "You also should wash one another's feet" (John 13:14)?*

We should give ourselves to service and love, no matter what our social status is. We should follow Jesus' example. When we are demonstrating God's love, even the dirty tasks reserved for the lowest people are not too low for us.

3. *Why is service to others important?*

No one person is more important than another. Jesus has served us first and following Jesus' example shows the world what he is like.

4. *Who can you serve today? How?*

This can be something done together—does your church need chairs stacked? Would the teachers at your local school appreciate encouraging notes and a treat? Or it can be done individually—do you have a family member that needs to be served when you get home tonight?

FOR FURTHER STUDY

Matthew 5:13-16, 23:11-12, 20:25-28; John 12:26;
Romans 12:9-13; Galatians 5:13-15; Hebrews 6:10-12.

PSALM 86:15

But you, Lord, are a compassionate and gracious God, slow to anger, abounding in love and faithfulness.

FELLOWSHIP—TAKING FRIENDSHIP UP A NOTCH

We often put pressure on ourselves to figure things out on our own and be independent. God actually made us to depend on each other! In his grace, he provides people to mentor us, encourage us, pray for us, and teach us. Today we look at the importance of fellowship and ways we can develop relationships with believers.

READ

Answer these questions after reading Luke 5:17–26.

1. *What did you learn in Luke 5:17–26 about the power of friendship?*

   Answers will vary. Friendship involves sacrifice. A friend meets a need I can't meet on my own. We can have faith that God can change the lives of our friends. He will act when we bring our friends to him.

2. *Why is fellowship important?*

There are some things we can't do on our own. We need encouragement and people to speak truth to us. We can each contribute in different ways.

3. *Who in your life can you have fellowship with?*

Reminder: fellowship is experienced with other believers who can build us up. Friendship with unbelievers is also important, but we are focusing on spending time with those who will strengthen our faith.

4. *How can you build relationships with other Christians?*

Brainstorm a list of ideas and then evaluate: are we actively building these relationships now or will that begin today?

FOR FURTHER STUDY

1 Corinthians 12:12–31; James 5:16.

EVANGELISM—IT'S FOR EVERYONE

Evangelism can sound intimidating, but it simply means "telling the good news." Instead of fearing spiritual conversations or believing that evangelism is for other people, we can ask God how he would like to use us to share his good news.

READ

Answer these questions after reading Acts 2:14–41.

1. *What does a "witness" do in a court trial? What does a "witness" talk about?*

   A witness tells what they have seen and experienced. They are a type of proof. They know something they can share for the benefit of others.

2. *What do you think it means to be a "witness" for Jesus? What kinds of things would you talk about?*

We can share what we know about Jesus and how he has changed us. We can talk about what is true from the Bible.

3. *Who can you share the gospel with?*

Write down a name of a person who comes to mind.

4. *Pray for that person and ask the Lord to give you an opportunity to share with that person.*

Before concluding today's study, take time to pray together for that person.

FOR FURTHER STUDY

Read about Peter before he had the confidence to preach about Jesus (John 18:15–27), and after Jesus reinstated him (John 21:15–17). Be encouraged that the same Peter was empowered by the Holy Spirit and was able to preach in Acts 2. Also read Psalm 105:1, Isaiah 6:8, and Matthew 5:14–16.

A WORK IN PROGRESS

As long as we are still breathing, God isn't done with us. We don't always see results overnight, but we trust if we are turning to him, he is transforming us. Don't be discouraged or overwhelmed in the process. God uses the process to refine us and draw us to him.

READ

Answer these questions after reading Ephesians 1:3–14.

1. *According to Ephesians 1:4, when did God choose you? For what purpose did he choose you?*

   Before the creation of the world, his purpose for us was to be holy and blameless in his sight and devoted to the praise of his glory (v. 12).

2. *How does God seal his promise to you? (See Ephesians 1:13–14.)*

   He gives us his Holy Spirit.

3. *Why is Jesus trustworthy? What did you learn about Jesus today?*

   He chose us before the creation of the world, he redeemed and forgave us, and he gave us his Holy Spirit. He keeps his promises.

4. *Ask God to give you "the Spirit and wisdom and revelation, so that you may know him better" (Ephesians 1:17).*

   This is also a great prayer to use as you start studying the Bible each day. Ask God to direct your study and prayers.

FOR FURTHER STUDY

Romans 12:1-2; Ephesians 4:17-32; 1 John 2:6.

HEBREWS 13:8

Jesus Christ is the same yesterday and today and forever.

WHERE DO I GO FROM HERE?

When Jesus left the earth, he gave his disciples the Great Commission. He instructed them to live intentionally and continue in their transformed lives. Today, make a "what's next" plan for further study and fellowship, and take time to celebrate what God has done through the course of this study.

READ

Answer these questions after reading Psalm 63.

1. *In what ways can you relate to the psalmist's desire to seek God and praise him?*

   This can be general or include specific verses that stood out.

2. *Reflect on the past forty days. How has your faith changed? How has your life changed?*

This will take a while! Review the book and specific questions to recall ways that God has been at work in you.

3. *How will you seek God this week?*

It's important to have a plan. We need to be intentional about caring for all our relationships, and our relationship with God is no different. Don't end this discussion without some concrete conclusions.

4. *What will you do to continue to grow in your relationship with God? Ideas: Talk to your pastor or small group leader about books or studies you can do. Pick a prayer partner. Decide to memorize a verse every week. Choose a time during the day to have time with the Lord.*

Maybe it's time to choose another person to walk through this devotional with. Then ... celebrate! Plan something fun or meaningful to end the study.

FOR FURTHER STUDY

Psalm 23; John 10:1–18.

DAILY ENCOUNTERS WITH AN ALMIGHTY GOD

"Jarrid Wilson reminds us that faith is easier than we assume, that grace is freer than we believe, and that God is more majestic than we know. If you're worn out from striving for God's affection, then Wondrous Pursuit is for you."
—Jonathan Merritt, contributing writer for The Atlantic; author of *Jesus is Better Than You Imagined.*

Learn more at KirkdalePress.com/Wondrous